T0106194

From God's Heart to Mine

FOR THE ENCOURAGEMENT OF YOUR SOULS

Yvette Kearns

authorHOUSE®

AuthorHouse™
1663 Liberty Drive
Bloomington, IN 47403
www.authorhouse.com
Phone: 1-800-839-8640

© 2010 Yvette Kearns. All rights reserved.

No part of this book may be reproduced, stored in a retrieval system, or
transmitted by any means without the written permission of the author.

First published by AuthorHouse 7/22/2010

ISBN: 978-1-4520-4835-2 (sc)

Library of Congress Control Number: 2010910895

Printed in the United States of America
Bloomington, Indiana

This book is printed on acid-free paper.

Testimonial

I began writing "poems" when the Lord began speaking to my heart and I began listening.

It started on Saturday, July 25, 1992 with a poem entitled "Nothing is Impossible!" I had been reading/studying Luke 1:37 and Matthew 19:26, when I heard the Lord tell me: "Sometimes it's rough, but I will sustain you".

I continued writing while listening to the Lord and have written many poems God has given me for whatever was and is going on in my life at the time.

I continued to write whatever God put in my heart and on August 16, 2002, when my twin boys were 4 months old; I was hit with a life changing, heart breaking and spirit breaking changing event in my life; and on January 17, 2005, the Lord continued to speak to me about forgiveness and began speaking to me about writing a poem entitled "Forgiveness". I began writing down all God said to me and all I'd said back to God. Yes, I had not forgiven and was not ready to forgive and did not want to forgive; nor did I want to hear God's voice or His Words. I argued with God, but I did what God said and finished the poem.

To be able to write and get God's Spoken Word on paper and to get God's voice heard, my voice heard, my feelings felt by others and encourage others at the same time is very humbling and up lifting. Because of this humbling and uplifting experience; I have been inspired to write and publish this book you are about to embark on.

If you feel you have no voice and you are in despair, but you hear The Lord say something...anything...I encourage you to write it down (make sure it lines up with the Word of God) and share it with others and with the help of the Lord Jesus Christ...it will be heard.

Dedications

First I dedicate this book to you; those that are reading "From God's Heart to Mine...for the encouragement of your souls". I dedicate this to you because your souls are the souls that God wants to reach forever and it is my prayer that through these poems your souls will be won.

Secondly, I am dedicating this book to my Husband, Mr. Dathan Kearns. Without his love and the many trials we've gone through; neither these poems nor this book would be possible to write. I love my Husband with all my heart and with the Love of the Lord Jesus Christ; without Christ's Love, I could not Love my Husband according to the Lord's Word.

Thirdly, I am dedicating this book to my Twins; Aaron and Michael Kearns. My children have made me the woman I am today. Without those two little gentlemen of mine, I do not know what I would do. They truly open up my eyes, my mind and my heart to what it truly means to be a mother and most importantly; a mother in Christ Jesus.

I'd also love to dedicate this to my Momma, "Ms. Jo", who I have received my writing skills from. She was an English Major in College and she loved to write. She went home to be with our Lord and Savior, Jesus Christ, right before my eyes on Thursday, March 22, 2001 and did not get a chance to meet the twins, read any of my poems or hear any of the songs that have originated from my poems.

I would also love to dedicate this to my Daddy, Mr. Joseph Williams. He has taught me a lot of wisdom and how to take care of myself on my own without anyone's help. He also taught me the ways of true life and how to live in this world. I also dedicate this to my Stepmother, Mrs. Arlene Williams. She has been an inspiration in my life since I was around 8 years old. Over the years she has given me countless advice and guidance in my life. She has shown me love and because of all she has done for me, I don't consider her my "Stepmother"...she is my Mother and I love her dearly. I never would have made it through many trials if it had not been for her.

I also would like to dedicate this book to the friends in my life who have help me in my everyday life and in all my times of need; Betina & Thaleus Wilcots; Mammanette (Jeanette Ruffin); Little Mammanette (Jeanette Howard); Terrilynn Bryant; Karen Wallace; Sherri Cummings; Lynn Whiting; Paula & Eric Milner; and to my Pastor & Dear Friend, Dennis Hackett, who has been a strong spiritual influence in my life and who has encouraged me in my writing poems by watching him with his song writing. I'd also like to dedicate this book to his wife; also my Dear Friend, Gerrie Hackett, to whom I have called upon many times for prayer and a Word from God. She has always been able to tell me what thus saith the Lord whether I want to hear it or not and for that; I thank her.

This book is also dedicated to all those I love and care about; of which the list would be too long to add to this book. Although, I can't name everyone, I love you all and I appreciate and thank you for your inspiration in my life. And in naming those people of which it would take the whole book, the first part of this would not be possible without a very special friend of whom I've known all of two years...thank you very much for giving me the inspiration and the extra push to go ahead and write the book, because there were many times I did not want to do it whether God put it in my spirit or not...so to that...I say Thank You!

A Very Special Dedication

This book is very lovingly dedicated to the memory of my Mother, Joann Elizabeth Acton. Or as she was most affectionately known, to all that knew her and loved her; as "Ms. Jo".

"Ms. Jo" was sadly taken from me/us on Thursday, March 22, 2001 in front of me; in our house; on her bed; in her bedroom. I watched and felt somewhat helpless as she took her last breath and as the paramedics' worked on her constantly to no avail. But I knew the same God she knows and I knew she would be in Good Hands at Home!

"Ms. Jo" is with the Father and I know we will all see her again.

"From God's Heart to Mine...for the encouragement of your souls" is lovingly dedicated to the Loving Memory of my Mother and our Sister in Christ Jesus…"Ms. Jo".

Contents

In Return

In return for a black, hardened heart, the Lord will give you a heart as white as snow and as soft as silk.

In return for your sins, The Lord will give you righteousness and eternal life.

In return for your mourning and crying, The Lord will give you comfort.

In return for meekness, you will inherit the earth. In return for confusion, The Lord will give you peace.

In return for hatred, The Lord will give you Love.

In return for spiritual hunger and thirst, the Lord will fill you. In return for delightfulness in the Lord, He will give you the desires of your heart.

In return for trusting in the Lord with all thine heart and acknowledging Him in all your ways, He will direct your paths.

In return for a pure heart, we shall see God.

So What Do You Have To Give?

Close your eyes; worship and think on these things.

Inspired by the Holy spirit-8/1/93-Written by Yvette Kearns

Lord I'm Seeking You

Something happened to me in the past that made me grow up too fast, but I continue going my own way trying to deal with it-day by day.

Even though I'm older now, I've got to find a way to stop the pain somehow.

Lord I'm seeking you.
Your Love, Your Strength, Your Peace.
Lord you know just what to do.

Your Word says Love covers a multitude of sins, but I can't find that love within. You Word says you give a peace that will pass all understanding, but somewhere in my soul it's lacking. Your Word says you are my Strength, my Rock and my Shield, but I sometimes feel I'm without You in an open field.

Lord I'm seeking you.
Your Love, Your Strength, Your Peace.
Lord you know just what to do.

Inspired by the Holy Spirit-2/18/94-Written by Yvette Kearns

My Thoughts
Listening & Speaking With My Father

One would think that I have learned by now that those who say they are your friends; are not true friends, but there is only One True Friend and that is Jesus.

He is a Friend; A Guide; A Provider; A Healer; A Good Shepherd; etc. And His Holy Spirit is Our Teacher. He has proven it time and time again, even 'til the end when He died for my sins and your sins.

No Greater Love hath No Man Than a Man Who Would Lay Down His Life For a Friend.

And yet we choose flesh; we choose people; unsaved people and saved people; people who know not Christ or profess to know Him, but don't really practice what they profess. These are the people we/I choose to call friends.

A Man That Hath A Friend Must First Show Himself Friendly...And There Is a Friend that Sticketh Closer than A Brother.

His Name Is Jesus Christ, the Son of God...He is God and it's time now to believe and Trust in Him and Him only.

Inspired by the Holy Spirit-8/8/95-Written by Yvette Kearns

The Lord Has Opened Doors
That The Adversary Can Never Shut

The Lord has opened a door that the adversary will try to shut at all times; every hour; every minute; every second; every situation; and ever circumstance, but they cannot because what The Lord has opened no man; no situation; no circumstance; no storm; nothing will be able to shut it.

But with all this we also play a part in this opened door He has for us because in all actuality; we are the main adversary. You see; we allow those doors to shut when situations arise and we forget about the Lord and His Word. We get angry; argumentative; abusive; we become fornicators; liars; cheaters; stealers; worry warts and we allow depression to take hold over us. We act out instead of relying on God's Holy Word...Trust in the Lord with all thine heart and lean not unto thine own understanding (don't do what you want in that moment; that situation; and in that anger...remember God's Word...keep it close to your heart at all times). In all thy ways acknowledge Him, He shall direct thy path (if you keep the Lord always in your heart and on your mind you will always keep that door open).

The Lord has opened the door of peace, but anger will try to shut it...will you allow it?

The Lord has opened a door of obedience, but disobedience will try to shut it...will you allow it?

The Lord has opened a door of truth, but lies will try to shut it...will you allow it?

The Lord has opened a door of faith, but worrying and depression will try to shut it...will you allow it?

The Lord has opened a door of Abundant Life (Life Eternal), but hate and disbelief will try to shut it...will you allow it?

Please trust the Lord in every situation, every circumstance, on your job, in your home, with your spouse, with your children, with your neighbor and especially with other saints.

Inspired by the Holy Spirit-9/22/99-Written by Yvette Kearns

Who Is This Man?

He is a friend that sticks closer than any brother. He's unlike any other.

He is Alpha and Omega, the Beginning and the End. He never changes with the wind, He's always straight and never bends.

He makes you to lie down in green pastures and leads you beside still waters. He speaks to the winds and the waves and He calms the sea. He rains on the just and the unjust, He does it for you and He does it for me.

He asked His Father for us to keep in His Hands never to be plucked away by anything or any man.

What Kind of Man is this who would lay down His life for His friend and who would hang on a cross, die and rise again?

Who Is This Man; This Friend; This What? This Who?

His Name is Jesus and He's Calling You!!!!

Inspired by the Holy Spirit-11/16/98-Written by Yvette Kearns

It's Not Your Will

It's not what you need; it's what I have. It's not what you want; it's what I'm going to give you. It's not your will; but it's My Will Be Done!

You say things aren't going your way, you're praying for a brighter day. I gave you strength to stand. Strength and truth to overcome any man. Instead you want to do things your way . You pray for a change in your situation and to that you cling, but take a look around, I'm not changing a thing.

It's not what you need; it's what I have. It's not what you want; it's what I'm going to give you. It's not your will; but it's My Will Be Done!

The change you seek for begins with you. Watch everything you say and everything you do. I have souls I want saved and lives that need to be changed. This can only happen when you abide by my rules. I am the Vine, You are the branch, and without Me you could not survive. So stop seeking counsel that is not of Me. Stop trying to do things on your own. Do you think I can't see?

It's not what you need; it's what I have. It's not what you want; it's what I'm going to give you. It's not your will; but it's My Will Be Done!

Inspired by Holy Spirit-11-30-98-Finished-12-5-98-Written by Yvette Kearns

What if God said, "Go!" Would You?

I had a dream I was a prostitute. Me and the other girl were on the street working and our pimp rolled up. He was fine, his car was fine and I was in awe. He got out the car and started talking about how if you want things, you have to do certain things to get them. Then it was just me and him, the other girl disappeared. He (the pimp)
Showed me a pair of sunglasses. He said, "you like those, huh?" "Here, touch 'em." Man, those were the best pair of sunglasses. Guess what, though? They were so simple, but they were smooth and went on easy. Then he said, "to get these (glasses) you got to go where cows (do something...he said, but I can't remember), but he gave me a suitcase, a raggedy coat, and a pair of glasses that glaucoma patients wear; and out of nowhere appeared a crowed of people, so I began walking down this narrow road, and they were laughing at me.

So what if God said, "Go!" Would you?

The Sunglasses represent Salvation: Salvation is so easy to get, if you believe.
John 3:16; I John 5:11 and John 6:47.

Remember the pimp said "if you want things, you have to do certain things to get them". The only thing you have to do to get Salvation is to believe on the one who died for you. JESUS. The smoothness of the sunglasses and the way they were so easy to wear is a symbol of God's Yoke and His Rest (Matthew 11:28-30).

Inspired by the Holy Spirit-Written by Yvette Kearns

I Am A Woman

I was taken from Adam's bones; created by God to be a help meet so man would not be alone.

I Am A Woman!

When I was born they shouted; "it's a girl, it's a girl"; with such joy; never knowing I'd be someone's toy.

Getting older now, but still a child; being told how pretty I am and what a good girl I am, while trying to make your next move go mild...humph...well, it worked.

I told no one because I trusted you. This couldn't be happening; no, not to me.

Getting older now with this rock on my shoulder; if someone found out it would become a boulder. I sheltered it in my heart and it caused me great pain.

With each relationship I had, I lost my grip, but I began to find comfort in men; all the while holding back the hurt as they grinned.

Until one day I found solace in a man who was born to die for the remission of my sins. This Man's Forgiveness causes me to forgive. The Man has put happiness in my heart and has encouraged my soul. He'll love me forever is what I am told.

His Name Is Jesus.
He gave His Life for me, now I live mine for Him.

I Am A Woman; A Woman Of God!
I forgive you!

Inspired by the Holy Spirit-3-23-03;Finished 3-27-09-Written by Yvette Kearns

Prostitution

Today prostitution is glamorized. It's made out to be something good. I can get paid more in an hour than the average woman makes on her "straight" job. I got the "wheels"; "the bling, bling"; "the ice"; "the crib"; all to show I'm making it, but I'm not.

I give out what I think is love to men that think they love me...humph...they don't love me; they love what I got. So it's a give and take relationship; they give... money, that is and, uh; I take...money, that is.

Some of us do it 'cause we have no choice; so we think. Some of us do it to put food on the table for our hungry kids, diapers and formula for those of us who have babies. Some of us do it to keep the lights, gas and cable on; but is there another way?

Well, I started talking to and listening to this woman named "Mary Magdalene". She said she was around when a Man named Jesus was walking the earth. See, she was from the times when prostitution was ugly. Women who did it were called "whores" and "harlots", and if caught, they were stoned to death; but today the most you'll get is jail time or, oh yeah, the ultimate outcome will be death; if you get AIDS or if some fool beats you to death. Anyway, she started talkin' 'bout how she was tormented by seven demons and how she had done a host of other things, but one day she met a Man named Jesus. When she met Him He said to her: "Thy sins are forgiven, thy faith hath saved thee. Go in peace".

There is a better way, a better truth, and a better life. Jesus is that way, that truth, and that life. No one can come to the Father but by Him.

So, have that same faith "Mary" had. Believe and He will make you whole.

Inspired by the Holy Spirit-Written by Yvette Kearns

A Hug

Absolutely nothing but Jesus and His

Holy Spirit wrapping their arms around me
Ultimately leading and guiding me to do what's right
Giving me reprovement, chastisement, correction, and God's Abundant Love.

Inspired by the Holy Spirit-12-30-04-Written by Yvette Kearns

Who's Sins Are Worse?
Christians or Unbelievers?

If Christianity was a crime, punishable by imprisonment, I often wonder if Law Enforcement could find any evidence against me. I believe some of the time they could and some of the time they could not.

The times when there would not be any evidence of Christianity are the times when my lying lips; filthy communication; foolish jesting, etc. would cause my prayers and any songs I sing to be as sounding brass and tinkling cymbals to God's ears, or when my stubbornness and disobedience becomes a stench in His nostrils.

Like the Children of Israel, I sometimes want more than what God has for me and instead of trusting in Him I create my own "god" out of melted gold. Are my sins worse? Yes! Actually, to God all sin is the same, there is no one sin worse than the other, but for myself, I know to do right and when I sin; it's as if I have crucified Christ again.

The Bible tells me in Numbers 15:29-31: "Ye shall have one law for him that sinneth through ignorance, both for him that is born among the children of Israel, and for the stranger that sojourneth among them. But the soul that doeth ought presumptuously, whether he be born in the land, or a stranger, the same reproacheth the Lord; and that soul shall be cut off from among his people. Because he hath despised the Word of the Lord, and hath broken His Commandment, that soul shall utterly be cut off; his iniquity shall be upon him".

Inspired by the Holy Spirit-1/9/98-Written by Yvette Kearns

Forgiveness

Lord how many times should I forgive the things they say and the things they do?
70 times 7 just couldn't by true.

It's too much you see; they did it to you; but this time they did it to me.

"So who do you think you are?" My Father said to me. "Did you suffer at the hands of man like I did?" "Did you hang on a tree?" Then He said to me...

"Forgiveness; if you don't forgive, I won't forgive you. You need to show them the same mercy I have shown to you. Forgiveness; have compassion, forbear and let go. Put on charity and My Peace will show."

"You trusted, loved, cared and gave a lot; or so you thought. What makes you think their souls you have bought?"

"I am the Father, I am the King and I tell you this day that love forgives all things."

"Love endures and is pure. Love suffers long and is kind, so keep this in mind; Love covers a host of sins and love will always be a friend."

Inspired by the Holy Spirit-1/17/05; Finished 1/18/05

You'll Never Know

Imagine sittin' with your Father and He turns to you and says, "I need you to die one day for the souls I've made. You see, they'll have their own will and they'll do as they please. They'll disobey and they'll leave, but you'll be the one who'll bring them back to Me; by the blood you'll shed on Calvary."

You'll never know and you won't understand why I gave my life for common man.

So I was born into a world that hated My Father and Me. I tried to teach them, I healed them and they still did not believe. Were the things I did so wrong? Were the Words I spoke so far gone? It was the easiest thing anyone had to do. Accept my Father and He'll accept you.

Can you imagine what it felt like to be asked of your Father to give your life for the human race? Can you see the look that was on my face? Well, I thought, Abraham was asked to sacrifice his son; he led him out in the field, put him on an alter, tied him down; it seemed as though it was done. My Father gave Abraham a Lamb hidden in a bush so he wouldn't have to kill his son and see his son's look. But I didn't have a Lamb hidden in a bush. My Father didn't give me anything to save my look. At first I asked for the cup to be taken from me, but then I realized, I had to die on that tree. There was no more sacrifice for man. I was the one; I was my Father's Plan.

At last I cried out: "Father, why have you left me?"; but I knew it was your souls I had to redeem, so I gave up the ghost and it was done. "Truly this Man was the Son of God", which was said by some.

I loved you; I love you, and I trusted my Father and His Plan. Will you love me? Will you trust Me? Will you trust My Plan?

You'll never know and you won't understand why I gave my life for common man.

Inspired by the Holy Spirit-2/11/05; Finished 3/26/07

Be Like Little Children

As I watch my twins interact; the way I should be in Christ becomes exact.

As children play on the playground, playing and fighting back and forth; it is clear to me then; I have not yet bared my cross.

Be like little children is what Jesus said. Convert yourselves and become as them; be humble like those little children and the same will be great in heaven.

Children play and are foolish. Children love and become angry but they forgive, they forget, and they long suffer.

Be like little children is what Jesus said. Convert yourselves and become as them; be humble like those little children and the same will be great in heaven.

Inspired by the Holy Spirit-3/13/05

Alone

I was formed in the womb Alone. My mother gave birth to me and there were doctors, nurses, my dad and family members; but I was born Alone.

I stand in the midst of people every day, my friends, my co-workers, my family; yet still, I am Alone. With some I share none of the same views, we don't believe in the same things, but with others I do share the same views and we do believe in the same things, but I am Alone.

When I am in trouble; when I am sad; when I am hurt; and when I am mad; some say: "Hang in there"; "I'm praying for you"; "You can make it"; but I am still Alone.

When I accepted Christ, though there were others around, I was Alone. When I was baptized, the preacher was there, the congregation was there; but I was still Alone.

I was born Alone and I will die Alone, but when I pray and study the Word of God; I am never Alone.

When I obey God's Word and do His Will; I am never Alone. God is with me when I love those that hate me for His Name Sake. God is with me when I forgive instantly because He Says so. God is with me in my obedience and in my disobedience. He Loves me unconditionally and will never leave me or forsake me; but the minute; the second; the hour I leave Him...I am Alone.

Inspired by the Holy Spirit-4/20/08

The Wound
I Peter 3:8-9 and I Peter 3:18, 21 and 22

When I was very young, you took something from me that could never be returned; there was a band aid placed on The Wound.

When I was older, you physically caused me pain and you caused me mental pain; there was a band aid placed on The Wound.

When I became a woman, you took my trust and broke my heart, which caused the other wounds to re-open; bleeding and festering, but before infection set in; I was reminded that there was one called Jesus who endured much more than the theft of His innocence, or physical and mental pain; or broken trust or a broken heart.

Jesus left His Throne and took on the sins of the World, which included me. He was betrayed with a kiss; spat on; beaten; and forced to carry His own cross on His bloody back, to be hung on.

At no time did he point a finger or open His Mouth to place blame or accuse. He asked His Father for our forgiveness and for our souls. He gave His Life and His Blood was shed so there would not be a band aid to place over the "sin" wound, but that it would once and for all be cleaned, disinfected, stitched, and healed.

Jesus did all that He did while He walked on earth to show us forgiveness, meekness; long suffering; kindness; compassion; patience; humbleness; obedience; and all though we/I believe in the Savior, Jesus Christ; we/I have not yet learned what He taught and still is teaching, but time is running out.

Will you/will I keep the band aid or accept the cleaning; the disinfecting; the stitching and the healing for The Wound?

Inspired by the Holy Spirit-1/17/09

Vengeance Is Mine

Vengeance is mine sayeth the Lord; I will repay. Just do as I have asked you and everything will be ok.

You're hurt, you're mad, you want someone to pay. I will do to him as he has done to me is what you can't say.

Don't say I will reward evil; wait on me, do what My Word says; continue in love and walk honestly every day.

Vengeance is mine sayeth the Lord; I will repay. Just do as I have asked you and everything will be ok.

Bless them that persecute you; that much you can do. Don't love with hypocrisy; hate evil; and get close to me...I'm Good.

Vengeance is mine sayeth the Lord; I will repay, just do as I have asked you; and everything will be ok.

Inspired by the Holy Spirit-1/19/09; Finished 3/24/09

For You

I was talked about and deemed a devil. I was spit on, slapped and beat 'til there was no more skin on my back. I carried that cross for you; then I died for you.

It was for you that I was born.
It was for you that I was slain.
It was for you!

Giving myself freely to you allowing you to choose; laying down my life, without strife; loving you unconditionally.

It was for you that I was born.
It was for you that I was slain.
It was for you!

I didn't want to do it, but My Father said it must be done. I cried Father forgive them and then it was done. I still pray for you and long for you to talk to me. Together forever is what I want us to be.

It was for you!

Inspired by the Holy Spirit-3-18-05-Written by Yvette Kearns

If I Gave You Forever

If I gave you forever, would you tarry here with me for one hour? If I gave our forever, would you spread My Word, My Love and My Power?

If I gave you forever, would you live your life for me? If I gave you forever, would you lay down your life daily?

If I gave you forever, would you win the souls of others? If I gave you forever, would you pray for your sisters and brothers?

If I gave you forever, it would still be too late, you would think you were done and then I'd come. I'd be there as quick as a light, just like a thief in the night.

Inspired by the Holy Spirit-4-17-05-Written by Yvette Kearns

Fear Me

Fear Me, Fear Me, I'm God Above.
Fear Me, Fear Me, I gave you My Love.
Fear Me, Fear Me.

Listen, you that seek me, I'm not in the pit you dug. My righteousness is very near and my salvation is here.

Though my arms will Judge you, on them you can trust. Look up to heaven and down to earth below. The heavens will go away and the earth will wax old, but my salvation is forever and my Righteousness is Gold.

Fear Me, Fear Me, I'm God Above.
Fear Me, Fear Me, I gave you My Love.
Fear Me, Fear Me.

Listen; you who know me; you that have my law in your heart. Fear not man, nor their reproach. Fear not the man who can kill your body, for he can't take your soul. Rather; fear Me, I can reveal what's hidden and what you think is not known.

Fear Me, Fear Me, I'm God Above.
Fear Me, Fear Me, I gave you My Love.
Fear Me, Fear Me.

Inspired by the Holy Spirit-4-17-05-Written by Yvette Kearns

God Is Here (Candlelight)

God is here, He is here, don't be afraid of His Candlelight. God is here, he is near, don't be afraid of His Candlelight.

His Candlelight is True and Just. He wants you to have it, it's a must. It's His Will, but you want your own.

You prayed and you waited, but it didn't turn out right. Did you pray the way God instructed or did you pray amiss? You want things for your pleasure, but you should be seeking Holy treasure. You should know God doesn't grant your every wish. He is here to make sure you complete His list.

Love your enemies, act Justly, Love Mercy, Walk Humbly with Him; forgive, forbear and live peaceably with all men. Pray God's Will and you'll never miss.

You keep trying to move that mountain and open that door, but God put that mountain in your way, and God closed that door you try to open every day.

God is here, He is here, don't be afraid of His Candlelight. God is here, he is near, don't be afraid of His Candlelight.

His Candlelight is bright and clear. Don't be afraid, draw near and He will draw near to you.

Do what God says resist yourself and the things you want. Humble yourself in His sight and He will surely lift you.

God is here, He is here, don't be afraid of His Candlelight. God is here, he is near, don't be afraid of His Candlelight.

Inspired by the Holy Spirit-4-17-05-Written by Yvette Kearns

G.O.D.   C.H.R.I.S.T.

Greater love hath no man than a man who would lay down His life for a friend.

Over all the world His Name was given above every name on which you can be saved...JESUS.

Died and rose from the grave all in three days; took the keys to death hell and the grave, without strife, so we could have eternal life.

Crucified, hung, bled, and died for you. What are you gonna do?

Honor His death, burial, and resurrection by accepting Him as your Savior.

Remember it was for you and your sins that He came and gave His Life.

Instantly receive Him and you will be restored. Saving Grace is what does it; you do nothing...just believe.

Together with Him is where you want to be when He comes back. He'll judge us, but afterwards we'll live with Him in eternity.

Inspired by the Holy Spirit-4-17-09-Written by Yvette Kearns

He Did It!!!

He hung the moon, the stars and the sun. He made the trees; the flowers; the grass; the animals and like a blanket, laid out the sky above and the sea below. He placed the mountains and valleys where they are and then he created man from the dust of the ground and gave him the authority to name each animal around.

When He was done He saw that it wasn't good for man to be alone, so he put him to sleep and created woman from his rib bone.

Adam and Eve is what He called them and He gave them a home He called Eden. They were innocent, pure and sinless. He showed them everything in Eden, but showed them one tree they could not touch or eat from. He told them the tree of knowledge of good and evil you shall not touch, for when you do our relationship is through, and you will surely die.

He is the one who allowed the woman to be alone when the Serpent began to speak with his cunning and crafty; speech, saying, "surely He did not say you will die, go ahead Eve, give it a try. Share with Adam too and you both will see that after you have eaten of this tree; here in Eden you still will be".

He is the one who knew she would listen to the Serpent and it would break His Heart that the two He created would soon depart. But all the while He had a plan to restore His Love with man.

He is the one who sent His only Son to take on the form of a man, to walk the earth and claim to be God's Son. He is the one who knew His Son would be betrayed with a kiss and beat on; while on His face they would spit.

He is the one who knew His Son would carry His own cross on His bleeding back. He knew He would be nailed to it and hung up to die.

He is the one who knew that to sacrifice His son was the only way to reconcile man with Him. He knew if man would believe in His Son, their sins would be forgiven and man would have eternal life. He would be our Husband and we would be His Wife.

There was no big bang, no big boom or crash. No evolution; from monkey to man. He did it; He did it all. He was the Word and the Word was with Him and the Word was Him. He made all things: without Him there would be nothing.

He is God; creator of this world and all that is in it. He did it; nothing and no one else! God did it; God and Him alone!

Inspired by the Holy Spirit-May-2009-Written by Yvette Kearns

Why Do You Cry?

My child your tears and spirit are blue. I told you I'd never leave you nor will I forsake you. Do you find that not to be true?

My child I see your hurt and I see your pain, but I also see that in me you have everything to gain.

My child I know your sorrows; your troubles; your worries, and that you have no hope for tomorrow. But in My Word, I have given you tools to overcome this life. Why Do You Cry?

Stand firm in the faith even when your world seems to shake. I am your rock, your foundation and strong tower. It is from me and My Word that you will gain power. Why Do You Cry?

Trust Me, delight in Me and on you My Love will shower. Every day will not be happy; Everyday will not be sad; but on My Word if you stand, you can be made glad. Why Do You Cry?

Do what's right in Me and walk justly according to My Word; pray always without stopping because I am watching. I see the good and I see the bad. I see the wrong and I see the right, but this battle is not yours; it's Mine to fight. Why Do You Cry?

Let me be your comfort and your shield from the rain; obey My Word and I'll take away your pain. It may not be now, it may not be tomorrow, but endure to the end and you shall have power. I'll give you a garment of white and a crown of gold if you only do what you're told. Why Do You Cry?

The pain in this life will not always last. Believe in me and it soon will past. The plan is already in motion. My Son has already died. You have accepted Him and are now walking in the light. So again I ask...Why Do You Cry?

On judgment day you will see and definitely know I cannot, will not and I did not lie. I love you, I gave my only Son for you and for you He died.

Why Do You Cry?

Inspired by the Holy Spirit-May-2009-Written by Yvette Kearns

Can You Hear?

Hey! I'm talking to you. Can you hear? I know your can cause I gave you two ears, but you're too stubborn, arrogant, you want to be your own man and on your two feet you want to stand.

"News Flash"; I didn't create you so you could be what you wanna be. I created you so you could serve me. Because you accepted my Son, your life is no longer yours, it is mine and you will do things my way and in my time.

Stop saying I want this; I want that; I'm not magic, I don't pull rabbits out of hats.

I am God; King of Kings; Alpha and Omega; the Beginning and the end and it is to my business you will attend.

There are souls that are lost whom I want found. The same Word you heard...I want them to hear that sound.

How can this be done if you refuse to do right? You fight against me every day with all your might. You won't pray, you won't preach. I don't really need you, I can make the rocks cry out if you won't, but I want to use you. You're my vessel; my living, walking and talking testimony to help others to see this salvation, eternal life thing is not phony.

Listen! I'm close by; I am near; Can You Hear?

Inspired by the Holy Spirit-Written By Yvette Kearns

Do You Know Him?

When you get there, will He say well done my child; you suffered for my Son Christ's sake and you suffered a lot? Or will He say depart from me; I know you not?

When you get there, will He say you're too dirty, you never confessed your sins; therefore, you can't come in? You never once accepted my Son, so now your time in front of me is done.

What will He say when you tell Him, but I was a good person and I did everything the right way. I never lied, I never cheated and I never stole. On that day, to that, He will say; but you didn't believe the Saving Grace story my Son told. You would not accept Him into your heart; from Him and from Me you decided to depart.

You did your own thing and went your own way, so from this day forward, in Hell you will stay".

Will you be the one who knows Him, the one who found and entered in at the straight gate and the Words of the Lord you believed and in your heart; Him you did take, or will you be the one to stand at the door knocking; saying "open the door, we have eaten with you, we have drank with you and you taught in our streets"; only to hear Him say, "I will not open the door, I don't know you and you don't know me. Go away workers of iniquity".

Will you be the one who took heed to the Son of Man, opened your heart let Him in, lived your life for Him and took a stand? Will you be the one who took up your cross daily to follow Him; the one who studied His Word; preached salvation to the lost so they too could make it in?

My brothers and sisters, the time is now to accept the Son and His Father; He's already showed you how. He told you that He so loved the world, he gave us His only son and if you believe in Him you would not die the death of those who believe not, but you would live eternally and by His side you will be.

That should be enough; enough for you to believe it's true. Don't be the one to be banished; be the one to believe in His Son and to know Him and for that he will definitely know you!

Times running out, He's coming back, Do You Know Him; Has He Forgiven Your Sins and Will You Make It In?

DO YOU KNOW HIM?

Inspired by the Holy Spirit-5/31/09-Written by Yvette Kearns

So Tired!!!

So tired of striving to do what's right, but ending up doing what's wrong. I know you're tired of my same old song.

So tired of struggling with myself I have no more fight, but I know I have to be pleasing in your sight.

So tired of trying to study and pray. I can't do it no more, I can't make it another day, but I need to consume your Word and with you I must stay.

So tired of trusting; forgiving; and loving. Only to have the trust broken; the forgiveness taken and the loving shaken. Not doing things your way is why my heart is aching.

So tired of going day to day and night from night with my spirit crushed and my chest tight. I'm sorry Lord, I can't do it, this battle I can't fight!

But when I felt I was done and it was over; you said, "my child I'm here for you, your tears are on my shoulders. I'll never be tired of your song and with me you can never do wrong. You don't need to struggle or fight, your heart is always pleasing in my sight".

"With study and prayer you will make it today and another day. Although your heart is aching, continue to trust, forgive and love; by doing this your mind is on things above".

"Though your spirit is crushed and your chest feels tight; this battle you will never fight".

"The battle is not yours it's mine and though you're tired; in me you'll find rest. Keep striving, struggling, fighting, forgiving, trusting, and loving...it's a day to day test".

"Take up your cross daily, I know it gets heavy and you may feel like putting it down, but always remember I don't get tired; I'll always be around".

Inspired by the Holy Spirit/6/5/09-Written by Yvette Kearns

Time Heals; Love Covers

They say time heals all wounds; give it time and let it go. But what will happen when God calls and Love, Mercy, grace and forgiveness you did not show?

God says love covers a multitude of sins; it keeps no record of wrong; when you love; you always win.

They say I need time to think; I need space; I can't even look at your face, but what will you do at the end of God's race?

God says love never fails; to prove that...on a cross His Son Hung; His Hands and feet nailed.

They say forgive, but never forget and hold on to it just in case. Pay them back and give them a taste.

God says Love does not envy; Love trusts and Love hopes. What will you do when God says, "why couldn't you cope"?

Time heals; but with that there's debt and deals. Deals and debts you can't pay; neither can you keep, especially on judgment day.

Love covers; it shields and it shines. Love is the action that will cause God to say they're/you're mine.

Search your heart and keep this in mind; Love is not proud; it is not self seeking; not easily angered; Love is patient and Love is kind.

Remember what Jesus went through, for you. Remember he never failed. Grace and Mercy He gave too. He gave you an example of how to act, and how you should be; you should take heed now; when God calls it'll be too late to see.

Inspired by the Holy Spirit-7/31/09-Written by Yvette Kearns

What Would've Happened?
What If?

What would've happened when spat upon; Jesus spit back? What would've happened when accused; Jesus accused them? What would've happened when at the water well, Jesus didn't get water nor to the woman would he have spoken to? What would've happened when in the garden, betrayed with a kiss; Jesus retaliated? What would've happened when made to carry His own cross; Jesus refused? What would've happened when on the cross, because he had all power; Jesus got off?

What if, when cursed out; you/I curse back? What if, when lied on and talked about; you/I lie and talk about them? What if, when a word of encouragement needs to be said you/I kept our mouths shut? What if, when trust has been broken; you/I trust no more? What if, when being attacked for Christ sake; you/I attack back? What if you/I don't pick up our cross daily, but put it down? What if, when you/I are tried because of our faith; will you/I deny?

What would've happened if God decided to let us perish and not give us His Son? You/I would not have existed and we certainly would not have gotten the chance to repent, receive God's grace or faith to believe. You/I would be lost.

What if every time you/I disobey because we want our way; Jesus washed His hands of us and removed our names from the book of life? You/I would die and not live again.

What would've happened? What if? Don't let your actions and/or words result in those two questions being asked.

BELIEVE, REPENT AND LIVE.

Inspired by the Holy Spirit-8/3/09-Written by Yvette Kearns

Don't You Worry! Don't You Fret!

Don't you worry, don't you fret.
I'm (God's) in control you can bet.

When you feel you can't make it; trouble around and you can't take it. Look to me;
I'm your answer. I'm God in control and there's no other.

Don't be like Peter when he walked on water with my Son; he lost the faith and was
doubting; and was ultimately done.

Remember I'm on the water with you.   You won't sink and you won't be drowning.

Don't you worry! Don't you fret!
I'm in control you can bet.

Inspired by the Holy Spirit, 3/29/09-Written by Yvette Kearns

Find the Joy in Your Situation

You may not have had the biggest house or the nicest clothes but guess what; Jesus was born in a barn; didn't even have clothes made with yarn. Soon before He left that farm there was a king who wanted Him dead, but from that the more about His Fathers work He breed. He hung out in the temples from the time He was a boy; teaching and preaching in the synagogues never playing with any toys.; And when he was gone a few days at a time he would be asked; "where were you my child"?; "we looked all over", but He replied, "I must be about my Father's work."

Jesus found the Joy In His Situation, but do we/I?

His situation was that soon He would hang on a tree. We keep complaining about this recession, but we never take the time to show appreciation. We never give a kind word when one is needed; we never give a smile or any help to the person who pleaded.

We say in our hearts he's/she's just gonna buy wine with it or I'm not making that much myself; but nary a thought like this came from Jesus. When He was called upon by the blind man and people tried to shut that blind man up...NO....Jesus stopped; opened the blind man's eyes so he could see and the mouths of those shutting the blind man up were closed.

Jesus Found the Joy in Every Situation. He went about His Father's business in every nation.

So before we/I complain about how much we don't have or how little we received on our pay checks; or how we feel about losing houses and jobs and cars; let's think on these things...Seek ye first the Kingdom of God and His righteousness; and all these things shall be added unto you. Take no thought for the 'morrow (what it will do for you), the 'morrow shall take thought for the things of itself.

Love this day; do what you should do in the name of Jesus this day and tomorrow will not need your help.

Find the Joy in Your Situation; Do God's Work While It Is yet Day!!!!

Inspired by the Holy Spirit-11/22/09-Written by Yvette Kearns

An Insight Into The Lessons Given By God for Various Circumstances and Situations that I have been Through. And am Still Going Through and am Still Learning

Now we/I are about to embark in the pleasure of God's spoken Word in Lessons He has given me to help me in the situations and circumstances I go through and continue to go through.

It is my hope and faith that you will read them and study them with your spiritual heart mind and soul.

Remember my sister/brother in Christ that God's Word will not go out void, but will go out and establish what He wants it to.

It is my hope and prayer that these lessons will touch your spirit; speak to your heart; admonish and reprove you with God's Love.

Love,

Your Sister In Chirst Jesus

Nothing Is Impossible!

Nothing Is Impossible With God!

Do Not Be Anxious for Anything!

Do Not Grow Weary and Loose Heart!

Sometimes it's rough, but I know you will sustain me Lord.

Luke 1:37: "For God nothing shall be impossible (no word from God shall be void of

        power.)"

Matthew 19:26: "But Jesus beheld them, and said unto them, **With Men This is Impossible; but with God All Things Are Possible**".

Inspired by the Holy Spirit-7/25/92-Written by Yvette Kearns

"Is Your Faith Dead?"

James 2:14-26
Vs. 14 – The answer is no. The Bible declares we must be hearers and doers, not just hearers.

James 1:23
Once we have been given the tools for the task, we must use them.

Luke 11:24-26
Here this house has been swept and garnished, but it's not being occupied, so the unclean spirit returns with seven other spirits. If that house had been occupied; they (the seven other spirits) could not have gotten in, which means when we study and practice God's Word; then when circumstances and situations in our lives arrive; we'll have The Word in our hearts and spirits and those "seven spirits" will not be able to occupy our thoughts; use our hearts and cause us to say and/or do the wrong thing.

Hebrews 6:7,8
Those that hear and accept the Word of God, are blessed (not with tangible/carnal things, but spiritually blessed). Those that don't are cursed (also not with tangible/carnal things, but spiritually cursed...they will not receive life eternal).

James 2:15-17
If someone is starving, prayer alone won't work for them, they need food also. It's the same as us having accepted Christ; it's not enough; for us, daily we must pray; read and study the Word of God, having spiritual minds and not carnal minds.

Romans 8:6
"For to be carnally (worldly) minded is death; but to be spiritually minded is life and peace."

I John 3:18
Love alone is dead. Without the showing of love together with speaking it; it's nothing. Love is an action, not just words by themselves. If we are hearing and not doing; if we are praying for and not giving to; if we are saying we love and are not showing; these then, are alone. We must hear and do; pray for and give; speak love and show it.

James 2:26
"For as the body without the spirit is dead. So faith without works is dead also."

Inspired by the Holy Spirit for the teaching of my soul and sharing with others.

"I Asked The Lord"

I asked the Lord for help. I asked the Lord to teach me to study, to pray, and to Love. I asked Him to help me hear His voice and to help me to be submissive to His Will and His Way. I asked the Lord to help me to diligently seek Him, that He may reward me spiritually. I asked the Lord to help me to be the wife the Word of God tells me to be; something I need a lot of help in. After I prayed, I started reading the Word of God; and one of the scriptures given to me for my Heavenly Father was:

Isaiah 41:10
"Fear thou not; for I am with thee: be not dismayed; for I am thy God: I will strengthen thee; yea, I will help thee; yea, I will uphold thee with the right hand of My Righteousness."

"Any Kind Of Love"?
Not Our Love, But God's Love

I John 4:12:20-21/I John 2:4
Don't be a liar, if you love God, love your brother.

Romans 15:1-2
Infirmities-Sickness-Feebleness=SINS
We must bear these things of the weak and not please ourselves. **How?** We can please ourselves in many ways: 1) When we are angry, we can tell them how we feel; 2) We can have an attitude; 3) We can treat them as though they were nothing. But, *vs. 2* tells us that we must please them *(the weak, our neighbor)* for their good to edification. We do this so that they will have knowledge of the Word, gain Wisdom, and Understanding. By doing this they will see the Christ in us.

Galatians 6:1; I Corinthians 4:21; II Timothy 2:24,25 *(also read the whole chapter)*; Hebrews 12:13 *(also read the whole chapter)*.
These scriptures tell us how to deal with the weak, the one who is slipping away. We must deal with them in the spirit of meekness and with love, considering ourselves. We must do these things so that they may be turned away from their sickness, their weakness and their transgressions.

Romans 15:7
We must receive one another as Christ received us. While we were yet in our sins He loved us and died for us. **Romans 5:8**

I Corinthians 8:9-13
Because we have freedom in Christ, we still need to watch what we do and say around the weak. *(Even when we are not around them!)* They will do what they see us *(the Strong)* do. We were that way once and sometimes still are. If we don't go to church, the will not. If we drink, they will think its ok too. *(These are tangible things)* Do nothing to cause the weak one to stumble.

Romans 8:6-9

Inspired by the Holy Spirit for the teaching of my soul and sharing with others. Written on 1/21/95; finished on 1/26/95. Praise God!

"My Fools, Make Me A Fool"

Philipians 2:13,14-"For it is God which worketh in you both to will and to do of [for] His good pleasure. Do all things without murmurings and disputing:"

My fool, in this, is thinking I can get out of situations the Lord has placed me in to do His Will. Not wanting to accept this, I become a fool. I become wise when I accept what He has given to me to say and do; and when I am able to realize:

Romans 8:28-"And we know that all things work together for good to them that love God, to them who are the called according to His purpose."

Jeremiah 2:5-8-"Thus saith the Lord, what iniquity have your fathers found in me, that they are gone far from me, and have walked after vanity, and are become vain? Neither said they, where is the Lord that brought us up out of the land of Egypt, that led us through the wilderness, through a land of deserts and of pits, through a land of drought, and of the shadow of death, through a land that no man passed through, and where no man dwelt? And I brought you into a plentiful country to eat the fruit thereof and the goodness thereof; but when ye entered, ye defiled my land, and made mine heritage an abomination. The priests said not, "where is the Lord?" And they that handle the law knew me not: the pastors [rulers] also transgressed against me, and the prophets prophesied by Baal, and walked after things that do not profit."

II Corinthians 3:5-"Not that we are sufficient of ourselves to think anything as of ourselves; but our sufficiency is of God;"

I am a Fool when I walk in my own ways and disregard the Lord, saying I don't need Him, I can do it on my own.

I Corinthians 1:18-"For the preaching [Word] of the cross is to them that perish foolishness; but unto us which are saved it is the power of God."

To do what God has commanded me to do will make me a Fool to the world. To do what the world would say, I should do would make me a Fool to Christ. I'd rather be a Fool for Christ than to be a Fool for the world.

Inspired by the Holy Spirit for the teaching of my soul and sharing with others. Written on 2/7/97…Praise God!

"The Will Of God Is Perfect...Bear Fruit!"

God has a plan for everything. His Will is perfect and good. And though we may not know what lies ahead, we are to trust God always and give Him thanks continually in all things. So you may hear scriptures like: ***Proverbs 3:5; I Thessalonians 5:18 and James 1:23*** And you think: Nothing is going to happen to me or you may not fully understand what those scriptures mean so you put them on the back of the shelf, and then: ***Jeremiah 11:19***-Almost like Job. We can't compare, but the way God tried Job is the way He tries us in our everyday lives.

Jeremiah 17:10-The Lord is the one who tries us. He is the one who allows the enemy to tempt us. God wants to see what we'll do and what we'll say. He wants to see what kind of tree we are, where we're planted, what kind of fruit we'll bare and what kind of substance we have, as though He doesn't already know.

Jeremiah 17:7,8-this tree is strong. It has substance. This tree knows:
Romans 8:28;Proverbs 8:19,21-And if this is true, why do we become like this tree:
Ezekial 19:10-14-WE MUST BEAR FRUIT!!

John 12:24-26;John 15:1-5;Romans 6:8-21-What kind of fruit did we used to bear?
Galations 5:19-21-What kind of fruit should we bear? ***Galations 5:22-26***-This is who we share our fruit with: ***Jude 12-13***-But we can help by bearing fruit ***Jude 20-23.***

Remember: ***Habakkuk 3:17-18***

This was inspired by the Holy Spirit from the events of 3-9-01 (My Husbands truck was stolen); 3-22-01 (My Mother died right in front of me from heart failure); and 3-28-01 (An ex-landlord sued my husband and I).

DID I BEAR FRUIT?

"Why Are You Afraid?"

__Matthew 14:25-32__-This was after the five thousand had been fed. **First Doubt:** The disciples thought Jesus was a spirit and they cried out for fear. **Second Doubt:** Peter wanted a sign…"if it's you Lord let me come out there too". **Third Doubt:** winds began to move the water.

We tend to focus on **the situation** or on **the circumstance** and not on the Lord.

__Matthew 8:23-27; Luke 8:22-25; Mark 4:35-41__-Our minds are on the situation; not on the Lord!

We doubt that the Lord is with us always.

__Matthew 19:16-22__-The rich man could not give his riches away for fear. Doubtful of what would become of him without his riches.

__Proverbs 3:5,6__-REMEMBER ALWAYS!

Inspired by the Holy Spirit for the teaching of my soul and sharing with others.

"Where Is Your Smile?"

When everything in your life is going good, *"Where Is Your Smile?"* is it on the outside or the inside? When your bills are paid, you have a job (a good job), your kids are behaving, your spouse is treating you well, you're eating good; just plain living good...*"Where Is Your Smile?"*** When nothing in your life is going good; *"Where Is Your Smile?"* When your bills are stacking up and not getting paid; *"Where Is Your Smile?"* When your cabinets are like "Old Mother Hubbard's"; *"Where Is Your Smile?"* When your kids are being disobedient; failing in school; doing drugs; or just plain going crazy; *"Where Is Your Smile?"* When your spouse tells you they've committed adultery; when they are not showing any compassion or consideration for your feelings, or when they are not helping around the house...*"Where Is Your Smile?"* Is it on the outside or the inside?

Where do you think Jesus' smile was when he prayed for us and then He had to die for us? Was it on the inside or the outside?
Job Chapters 1 and 2-We know from scripture that we are to be sober and vigilant because our adversary walks about as a roaring lion seeking whom he may devour. **(I Peter 5:6-8).**

Job 5:1-2-Sometimes friends, relatives and our sisters and our brothers in Christ tend to steer us the wrong way because they put themselves in the situation without seeking God first. Talking to friends, relatives and our sister and brothers in Christ are good, but they must also know where their smiles are. ***Job 5:8-11 (James 4:7-11).*** Your smile shouldn't vanish because you think God has done you harm by whatever you're going through. ***Job 5:17-27***

If your trust is in God and what He has done for you; not earthly or eternally, you should always have a smile. But where? ***Psalms 1:1-13; Jeremiah 17:5-8***

As we go through our problems, as we call them, we tend to question god. Why? Why me Lord? Where are you (Lord)? Why have your forsaken me? What have I done to deserve this?, etc. We never ask..."Lord what is it that you want me to learn? Or What is it about myself you want me to change?" ***Job chapter 38-42:6***

So ***"Where Is Your Smile"?*** If you have accepted Christ as your Savior, it should be on the inside so that it will show on the outside. When things in our lives are going good it's easy to **smile**, but the most important **smile** is the **smile** that comes from being obedient. Believing in God's Word, obeying God's Word, knowing that sins are forgiven and we have eternal life. We should be seeking things **above, not on earth.** ***Psalms 34:1,3,4,8,10 & 14; Job 13:15; Habakkuk 3:17-19***

So God asks you again...*"Where Is Your Smile?"*

Inspired by the Holy Spirit for the teaching of my soul and sharing with others.

"We Are Not Here To Receive Rewards From Man"

As children, some of us were often rewarded with some type of reward whether verbal or tangible. They often sounded like this: "Good job"; "I'm proud of you"; or we would get rewarded with sweets; toys, etc. Having these rewards as children conditioned us to want to receive the same type of rewards from "Man" in whatever we do in our lives, whether its school; church; work; home; or just in our everyday lives.

Have you ever felt like you did a good job, but others got credit or received a plaque, a certificate, or some type of "worldly" recognition, and you got nothing: If we tell the truth or be truthful with ourselves, the answer should by yes! I know I've felt like that, but then God spoke to me and reminded me that I was not here to gain rewards from Man, but to show God's Love, Mercy and righteousness to man to receive the rewards God has for me. Not a tangible reward, but an incorruptible reward. Do you want the world's rewards and/or acceptance or do you want God's?

Ephesians 6:1-8-This tells us that even as children we are to be obedient; why? Because "this is right". It instructs Children to honor their father and mother that it may be well with the children. It instructs parents not to provoke children to wrath, but to bring them up in the nurture and admonition of the Lord. If parents don't adhere to this, the Bible tells us in ***Colossians 3:21***-that provoking instead of nurturing and admonishing will discourage them.

If both the child and parent are obedient to God's Word they will receive a reward.

Colossians 3:22-25-This instructs us all whether we're on our jobs and have bosses or at school and have teachers, etc., to obey those masters; not to please them, but to simply please God. We should do this from the heart and not just to be seen of "Men", noticed and recognized, but to show "Men" and so they'll know we belong to Christ and have Salvation.

Colossians 3:1-17-If we are risen with Christ, we should not be seeking things of this earth. We should not be looking for tangible rewards whenever we feel we've done a good job at school, church, work, home, etc. We should always be seeking those things that are above. Our minds should always be set on things above not on earth. To do this we need to put off evil things and put on God's Mercy, His Kindness, His Humbleness, His Meekness, His Longsuffering, and we need to put on His Forgiveness to forgive others as He has forgiven us. We must, above all those things, put on God's Love and let His Peace take over our hearts. We must do these things and allow the Word of God to dwell in us, all in the Name of the Lord Jesus, not in the name of "man".

Titus 2:9 thru 3:1-7-In being obedient and denying ungodliness, etc. Don't give up!

I Peter 2:18-25-Being subject to our masters (mangers, supervisors, teachers, parents, pastors, etc.); not only to the good but also to the bad; this is acceptable to God. Jesus did it when He suffered for our sins. It was nothing we did, but He died for us. He definitely suffered wrongfully..

"We Are Not Here To Receive Rewards From Man"
Part II

How Much More Will You Suffer Wrongfully?

OUR REWARDS!

I Corinthians 9:25-We will receive an incorruptible crown while the world strives to receive a corruptible crown.

Ephesians 6:8-Whatever good thing we do unto Christ, not unto man, we will receive the same from the Lord.

Philiippians 3:14-The prize of the High Calling of God In Christ Jesus: An Eternal Prize.

Remember, if we profess Christ and to be children of God; don't seek "Man's" rewards; don't seek things on earth, but rather seek things above and strive for God's Rewards.

Seek the things that are above, not the things that are on earth!

Inspired by the Holy Spirit for the teaching of my soul and sharing with others; written, May of 2008.

Well my friends, here is another insight into my life, my heart, my situations, my sins, and my triumphs through Christ Jesus.

I share these experiences with you in my poems in hope and prayer that you will learn through the Bible and through Christ how you should react when problems of everyday life comes before us.

Remember, in Christ Jesus, we should always show Christ no matter what; anger, unforgiveness; unkindness; no love; no peace; whatever you experience on a daily basis is truly a test of your Faith and as a Child of God we; you; and I must always try to let Christ Shine through every circumstance and situation we may think is bad and believe that God is working it out for our good…if we; you; and I are obedient to His Word and do/act according to His Will.

Please read these next set of poems prayerfully and take them to heart. Learn from them, pray and believe that God is still on His Throne; He will never leave you nor forsake you. It is we; you; and I that leave and forsake Him every time; but just like the prodigal son…God is always standing there with open arms when we come back home.

Love,
Your Sister In Christ Jesus

"Love Infinity?"

There was a time when you were my all and my everything. You made me feel like I was more than a play thing. You were my all and I thought I was yours; you made me feel more than ten feet tall.

The first date was great. You treated me like I was the only one on earth. Considering what I felt you saved me from and where I'd been in my life; you were my rebirth.

You constantly complimented me; showered me with small gifts and flowers; you even dedicated three songs to me. With you I felt safe and free. We could talk about anything all day and all night; no worries about anything and we never had a fight, but soon it ended. Was it me or was it you? Who pretended this "Love Infinity"; who ended it?

What have I done to make you have ill will toward me? Is this "Love Infinity"; or is this a "Love Reality"?

I thought you liked my loud and boastful personality; but it turns out that I have become an embarrassment suddenly.

What did I do to cause you to stray? Was it not enough lovin' everyday? What is it about me and my body you don't like that caused you to entertain extra activities to do on certain days and nights?

What happened to the man I once knew? Maybe it's me who's changed and just can't see that this may not be "Love Infinity". The man I live with today, I do not know and maybe the woman you live with, you don't know and can't believe that her love may not be "Love Infinity". Is it you or is it me? Is this "Love Infinity"?

Your actions and verbal accounts have placed me in a very dark place in my mind and in my heart; a place that even I think Jesus is having a hard time pulling apart, but I know if any man can; He can do it; cause you see...His Love is Love Infinity.

When He asked His Father for my/our souls and died in my/our place; hanging on that tree; that was Love Infinity. When He was beaten, spat on and betrayed...He said, "Father forgive them for they know not what they do"; and when the man was ordered to carry His cross for Him; that was Love Infinity.

When Jesus said that if you confess and believe in me, you will live with Me for all eternity; that was Love Infinity.

Although, I'm still in this dark place I allowed you to put me in; having crazy thoughts of how it could all end...never waking up again; some kind of way I think about what Jesus did for me and then I say; "NO...your love is definitely not Love Infinity!"

Inspired by the Holy Spirit for the teaching of forgiveness; love; kindness; humbleness; obedience; patience; and virtue for myself & sharing with others; written, October 31, 2009

"In My Despair...I Had A Friend"

In my despair; I felt as though I was in disrepair. My heart was shattered and my spirit was scattered.

In my despair, I called a friend...I shared some things of which I can not to this end extend, but the things I shared caused concerned panic and shock; which lead to paramedics, counselors and a lot.

In my despair; I told someone who said, "you have people that love you; God loves you and He's there"; but He was not...in my despair.

During the chaos; there were two people that God revealed Himself through and that's when I knew; I knew God was there; even in my despair.

In my despair, I spoke to a friend who admonished and reproved me by the Word of God in a loving way, but it felt like this friend was angry with me; but this friend just wanted to remind me of in Christ who I should be.

So to you; whom I am writing to and to you who are reading this; I say to you: if you are ever in despair, and your heart and spirit leads you to believe that God is not there; I admonish you to remember God's Word; which will never go out void. He said He'd never leave you nor forsake you. God has told us of His forever Love but we must; as the Word says look on things above and not on things on this earth, which sometimes causes the most pain (ourselves).

In my despair, a friend reminded me of who I am in Christ and who I should continue to be in Christ with the way I live my life.

In my despair, a friend told me to focus on repairing me according to God's Word and to never let anyone take me away from God's Love.

To you I say, as a Sister in Christ and as a friend; whether or not you're in despair, always remember and forever engrave it in your heart that God will always be there; He will be you Love and your Friend 'til the very end.

Inspired by the Holy Spirit for the teaching of forgiveness; love; kindness; humbleness; obedience; patience; and virtue for myself & sharing with others; written, November 7, 2009.

"Your Standard"
Crushes My Heart and Tears My Soul

I'm having a problem with the standard you've set for me; you want me to be shut up and closed in, but I want to be free; free to say how I feel without being criticized; free to tell you what's inside my heart without being patronized.

The standard you've set is impossible you see, 'cause since the day we met; I've always been me.

Through time I've tried to change some things in me; about me, but you have taken them for granted and have not seen. Instead you attack me. You harsh words are just too tough.

You were my savior, my strength and my best friend; but the things you have done and the things you have said has somehow brought that to an end. I have forgiven (or so I thought) you over and over again. I've even apologized and from you received no amends.

God has said to me; forgiveness is the key; be like My Son and let it be, but I didn't die on that cross; I'm a human being, you see. I haven't reached perfection; I'm allowing you to cause me to become the woman God did not call me to be.

I cannot seem to win you over (although I try) with a meek and quiet spirit because you have broken my heart and spirit and God's voice...well, I've allowed you to cause me not to hear it.

I have no fight left; I can't fight you; I'm through with it. With your extra activities...I can't compete.

I'll keep praying and trying to be the best Christian I can, cause after all it is my own salvation that is in God's hand. You don't hold that; you never have. You may have power of words to break my heart; but I won't wait on you to mend it; no that's not where I'll start. I'll start and continue with God; He's the one who heals my soul and gives me a fresh start.

So you keep doing what you do and maybe someday with God's Grace; again we'll love each other the way we're supposed to according to God's Will.

Inspired by the Holy Spirit for the teaching of forgiveness; love; kindness; humbleness; obedience; patience; and virtue for myself & sharing with others; written, September 5, 2009.

"Let's Go Back! Can We?"

Let's go back in time when I was yours and you were mine. I thought we were each other's world; no other guys and no other girls; but my love; my heart, and my soul you have taken. I put all my trust in you and you left my world shaken.

I have allowed you to take my trust; destroy my faith and demolish my hope.

I should never have put you on that pedestal; so high. I should have remembered you weren't and aren't God; you're just a guy.

When you fell; I fell twice as hard and have not gotten back up, so I put up a guard. Not a spiritual one as I should have, but a carnal one which is very bad. This carnal guard allows me to pretend I'm someone else and it causes me to lash out at you; against everything you say and everything you do.

My spiritual guard would remind me that love never fails and love is not easily angered; but because of my carnal guard; my heart, I've allowed you to nail.

At times I feel like a wounded animal left on the road to die every time I allow you to put the nails in my heart; I hear the lies.

I need to go back in time when I was with God and gave Him all my time. I need to go back and put God on that pedestal because He'll never fall; then I won't have to. See in my heart I esteemed you high, but God has allowed all this to happen to show me why; why I should not put my faith and trust in man; but rather I should and I must trust in God and put my heart in His Hands.

Let's go back in time, when I was God's and He was mine. No others before Him and I gave Him all my time.

Inspired by the Holy Spirit for the teaching of forgiveness; love; kindness; humbleness; obedience; patience; and virtue for myself & sharing with others; written, September 5, 20009.

Aaron & Michael's Corner

Well I am now going to invite you into a journey through a child's heart and mind; a heart and mind that God used to speak through.

My Twins, Aaron & Michael both wrote poems. At first they were writing them on their own, but after listening to them read the poems, I assisted them...so in a since I co-wrote their poems. My two sons wrote these poems on their own listening to the Words of God that were placed in their hearts.

God can and will use anyone and anything to get His Word out into the souls of others and I believe He used my sons for that same reason.

I ask you to prayerfully read these poems, which were written by children. Ponder them, pray and seek the Lord.

Love,
Your Sister In Christ Jesus

"Jesus Be My Friend"

Jesus be my friend now.
I need you to show me how; how to love my brothers and be a good student and son.

So Jesus be my Friend
I need you to understand
I need help now
Please show me how; how to obey my parents, love my enemies and pray always.

Jesus you said you'd never leave me nor for sake me, so shape me and make me the way your Word says I should be.

Inspired by the Holy Spirit; written by Mr. Aaron Kearns on 4/24/09 @ 6 years old. Co-written by Yvette Kearns

"Darkness In My Head"

Darkness is in my head. God help me, I need you right now.

The devil is trying to get me in trouble. Lord I need your help on the double. He's (the devil) seeking whom he may devour. Lord it might be me. Please give me your power, it's your love that over me needs to shower. Lord this is my plea; help me.

Darkness is in my head. God help me, I need you right now.

Inspired by the Holy Spirit; written by Mr. Aaron Kearns on 4/24/09 @ 6 years old. Co-written by Yvette Kearns

"Be A Leader"

How do you be a good leader?
You got to be a good follower to be a good leader.

My teacher told me to sit in my set, but I didn't listen; I stood to my feet.

My teacher told me not to talk, but I opened my mouth and the words started to walk.

How can I lead if I cannot follow? It might seem that my brain is hollow.

I need to listen to my teacher so I can be a good leader.

How do you be a good leader?
You got to be a follower to be a good leader.

My teacher told me to complete my math, but I didn't; I did only half.

My parents told me to keep my hands to myself, but I didn't I touched someone else.

My Dad told me not to mess anything up, but I did, I messed with His cup.

How do you be a good leader?
You got to be a follower to be a good leader.

Jesus was and is the ultimate leader. When I/we learn to follow Him and when I/we do follow Him; that is when I/we will be great leaders.

Inspired by the Holy Spirit; written by Mr. Michael Kearns on April of 2010 @ 7 years old. Co-written by Aaron Kearns, Dathan Kearns & Yvette Kearns.

Ms. Jo's Corner

Once again I am taking you through another journey through the heart of someone else God spoke to and told this woman of God to write it down.

I have been compelled by the Holy Spirit to share with you what this woman of God wrote and how much in love she was with Jesus Christ.

My Momma, Ms. Jo, is with Jesus now and she now knows what we are all waiting to find out.

I invite you into her heart and spirit as the Lord spoke to her.

Once again, I ask you to prayerfully read these writings, ponder them, and seek God always.

Love,
Your Sister In Christ Jesus

"My Momma; Ms. Jo"

My Momma was a saint because she believed that Jesus Christ was and is the Son of God. She believed that Jesus Christ was and is God. She believed that He died on the cross and rose again for our sins.

My Momma had a good heart, she had a kind heart and she would try her best to do what she could to help anyone, but she could also be a "pistol". It took a lot to make her angry, but when she was; she was very angry.

My Momma, when she accepted Christ, would be the one who could calm my anger, my fears and my loneliness. We didn't always get along, but when I needed her she was there. But was I ever there when she needed me? Not always! But I loved my Momma with all my heart. She taught me how to sing and she taught me kindness.

My Momma wasn't always perfect but she was made perfect in Christ.

You see, the only thing that sets us apart from the sinner is that we are sinners saved by Grace. God gave us the Grace and Faith to believe in His Son. We did nothing. We are the same as those who don't believe. We have the same sins, the same sinful thoughts, the same lusts, etc., but we believe that Jesus Christ was the name that was given above all names. And my Momma sho nuff believed that Jesus Christ was her way, her truth, her life and He is the way, the truth and the life and no man can come to the Father but by Him! Jesus.

My Momma was a saint; not because of anything she said or did for anyone. She was and is a saint because she believed that Jesus Christ was and is the Son of God and that He came to earth to die on a cross for our sins and rise again so that we could be reunited with the Father.

Are you a saint? Do you believe?

Inspired by the Holy Spirit and memories of my Momma, Ms. Jo

Thoughts Written By Ms. Jo
Given to Her by the Holy Spirit

With Christ as my model of humility and service, I can enjoy a oneness of purpose, attitude, goal and labor.

With Christ as the center of my life, there's NO NEED TO WORRY! But I do sometimes, especially about bills...why? I don't know yet, maybe my faith is not as strong as it should be.

Philipians 4:6 tells me to be anxious for nothing, but in everything by prayer and supplication with thanksgiving let your requests be made known unto God.

I am not going to worry. I am really going to make a conservative effort on this matter. Worry is a sin; that means I am constantly out of the Will of God, which I don't want. I want to trust and obey.

Isaiah 30:15...in quietness and trust is your (my) strength.

Inspired by the Holy Spirit in the soul of Ms. Jo on 1/31/94-Written by Ms. Jo

More Thoughts Written By Ms. Jo
Given to Her by the Holy Spirit

I cried unto the Lord with my voice and he heard me out of His Holy Hill.

Give ears to My Words oh Lord Harken unto the voice of my cry.

I will praise thee with my whole heart in thee do I put my trust.

Have mercy on me oh Lord. Cast me not away from thy presence.

My cry is not only for forgiveness of my sins but also for the healing of my cancer. Have mercy oh Lord harken unto the voice of my cry. I am weary with my groaning, my pillow is covered with tears. My eyes are tired and my spirit is weak but I will continue to bless your Holy Name; for you are worthy to be praised. I will bless the Lord at all times His Praise shall continually be in my mouth.

In my distress I called upon the Lord and cried unto my God. He heard my voice out of His Temple and my cry came before Him, even unto His ears.

Inspired by the Holy Spirit, and the cries of Ms. Jo during her fight with cancer.

"The Way You Keep Me"

The way You keep me; bless me; have prepared a place for me.

The way You Opened my eyes; suffered so that I might be saved.

Thank you Jesus!

What would I be without You? I'm so Glad I'm Yours.

Inspired by the Holy Spirit-Written by Ms. Jo-11/25/98

"When the Lord Allowed Me to See 52 Years of Age"

When I reached 50 years of age, I thanked God and that was fine.

When I reached 51, I thanked God for saving my life by getting all the Cancer. I thanked Him for Brenda and Loma Linda.

When I reached 52, I was even more blessed. Veronica's change has come, Dathan treats me better and Yvette is not bitter toward me anymore. This was my best birthday.

The WHOLE family was together. Yvette cooked; bought me a beautiful opal ring with a little diamond. Veronica bought this book I'm writing in and we had a birthday cake that said:

PRAISE THE LORD!
YOU'RE 52!

Thank You Lord!

Inspired by the Holy Spirit-Written by Ms. Jo to show her praise and thanks to the Lord!

"This Morning"

The day is crisp and clear-I opened all the windows to let the apartment air out-The wind brings to mind a cleansing (of the city)-like when we read the Word, we are chastised, we repent and then we're cleansed.

Help me Lord to be cleansed of those things that are not like you. Even though the above thoughts were from my mind, I pray Lord they are also from my heart.

Philippians Chapter 1
Paul shows that even being imprisoned for preaching the Gospel has helped people spread the Word of God-by Paul not being down and out shows his love for Christ.

Philippians Chapter 2
We should all be of one accord, one mind; humble ourselves and be obedient as Jesus did-being born a man and dying a criminal's death-Do all things without mumbling or complaining so that your light will shine among those that are not saved.

Inspired by the Holy Spirit-Written by Ms. Jo-11/27/96

"Listening to a Song"

I was listening to a song called "It's Good to Know the Lord"; and I thought about the men of our congregation and Pastor Hackett's song came to mind:

"WHY WON'T THEY COME"

After knowing the Lord, His Goodness and how He saved, you; how could you go your own way?

"PRAY FOR OUR MEN!"

Inspired by the Holy Spirit-Written by Ms. Jo-3/29/97

Well, I'd like to take this time to thank all of you for joining me on this journey of poems and lessons. This journey for the saved (the believer) should have reproved; admonished; chastised; corrected you and showed you God's Perfect Love for you in your life in whatever circumstance you may be going through.

For the Unsaved (the unbeliever); It is my prayer that this journey has opened your heart and your spirit to God's Word and His Perfect Will for you, which is:
II Peter 3:9 - "The Lord is not slack concerning His promises, as some men count slackness; but is longsuffering to us-ward, not willing that any should perish, but that all should come to repentance".

Therefore take heed:
John 3:16 – "For God so loved the world, that he gave His only begotten Son, that whosoever believeth in Him should not perish, but have everlasting life".

It is my sincere prayer and hope; that if by going through this journey with me you have not softened your heart that you will in time. Don't be as Pharaoh was and harden your heart against God. There is no other way to come to God. Not by Jehovah, not by Buddha, not by Allah, or any other "man" or "thing" there is only one way to come to God and that is:

John 14:5 & 6 – Thomas saith unto him, Lord, we know not whither thou goest; and how can we know the way? Jesus saith unto him, "I am the way, the truth, and the life: no man cometh unto the Father, but by me."

Acts 4:12 – Neither is their salvation in any other: for there is none other name under heaven given among men, whereby we must be saved."

Philippians 9-11 – Wherefore God also hath highly exalted him (Jesus), and given him a name which is above every name: That at the name of Jesus every knee should bow, of things in heaven, and things in earth, and things under the earth; and that every tongue should confess that Jesus Christ is Lord, to the glory of God the Father".

So for the last time I take you on one last journey in prayer that you will understand how very important it is to believe; repent; and turn from your sins.

I pray that this book has touched your hearts and souls as God wanted it to.

Love,
Your Sister In Christ Jesus

"Irreplaceable? No You Are Not.
The Rocks Will Cry Out"

I've tried telling you since time began, but you always turn a deaf ear to me; so guess what? I'll use a tree.

I tried to tell you My Son was coming and again you closed your ears to my voice; so guess what? I'll use an animal of my choice.

Do you realize how powerful I am? I made you from the dust of sand. Do you think you are irreplaceable and I can't do without you?

I can't stand it anymore watching you strut about; so guess what? I'll make the rocks cry out.

If you don't tell someone quick about how I gave you My Love and My son, which was and is a gift; it will be too late; I'll let you become reprobate. Because, see, I don't really need you to get my point across, especially if you don't want to obey... and to think...I let My Son die on that cross.

You're not irreplaceable; you never have been and you never will be. Don't get me twisted; you don't have to speak for me. But watch out 'cause sooner than you think; the rocks will cry out.

Jesus is the name given above all names by which men can be saved. He is the truth; the way and the life; no man can come to Me (the Father-God), but through Him.

So, now tell me, are you irreplaceable? Do you think you will win with sin?

The rocks will cry out; if you don't, but by then it will be too late and the world will end.

Inspired by the Holy Spirit for the admonishing and chastising of our souls-11/28/09

63

The End

Or Is It?

About the Author

Having a unique voice, through my poetry, is a very humbling experience and to hear God speak and to be able to share what He has said unto me with others is indescribable. As an author my unique voice will bring encouragement, edification, and a new found love for God's written Word. He or she after reading just one of my poems will want to open the Word of God immediately; or they may decide to start opening God's Word, if they have not.